INTRODUCE YOUR LITTLE ONE TO THE WORLD OF ANIMALS WITH OUR HIGH-QUALITY, HIGH-CONTRAST BOOK. FILLED WITH CAPTIVATING BLACK AND WHITE PHOTOS OF WILD AND DOMESTIC ANIMALS, THIS BOOK PROVIDES VISUAL STIMULATION THAT AIDS IN THE DEVELOPMENT OF COGNITIVE SKILLS IN SMALL CHILDREN. LET THEM GET TO KNOW THEIR NEIGHBORS AND FRIENDS IN A WHOLE NEW WAY.

HELLO BABY, LET'S START OUR ADVENTURE

CAT

DOG

COW

HORSE

GOAT

SHEEP

PIG

RABBIT

MOUSE

HEN

DUCK

RAVEN

OWL

EAGLE

PENGUIN

MONKEY

GORILLA

KOALA

PANDA

WOLF

FOX

HIPPO

RHINO

GIRAFFE

ELEPHANT

ZEBRA

SKUNK

LEMUR

TIGER

LION

LIZARD

SNAKE

THE END